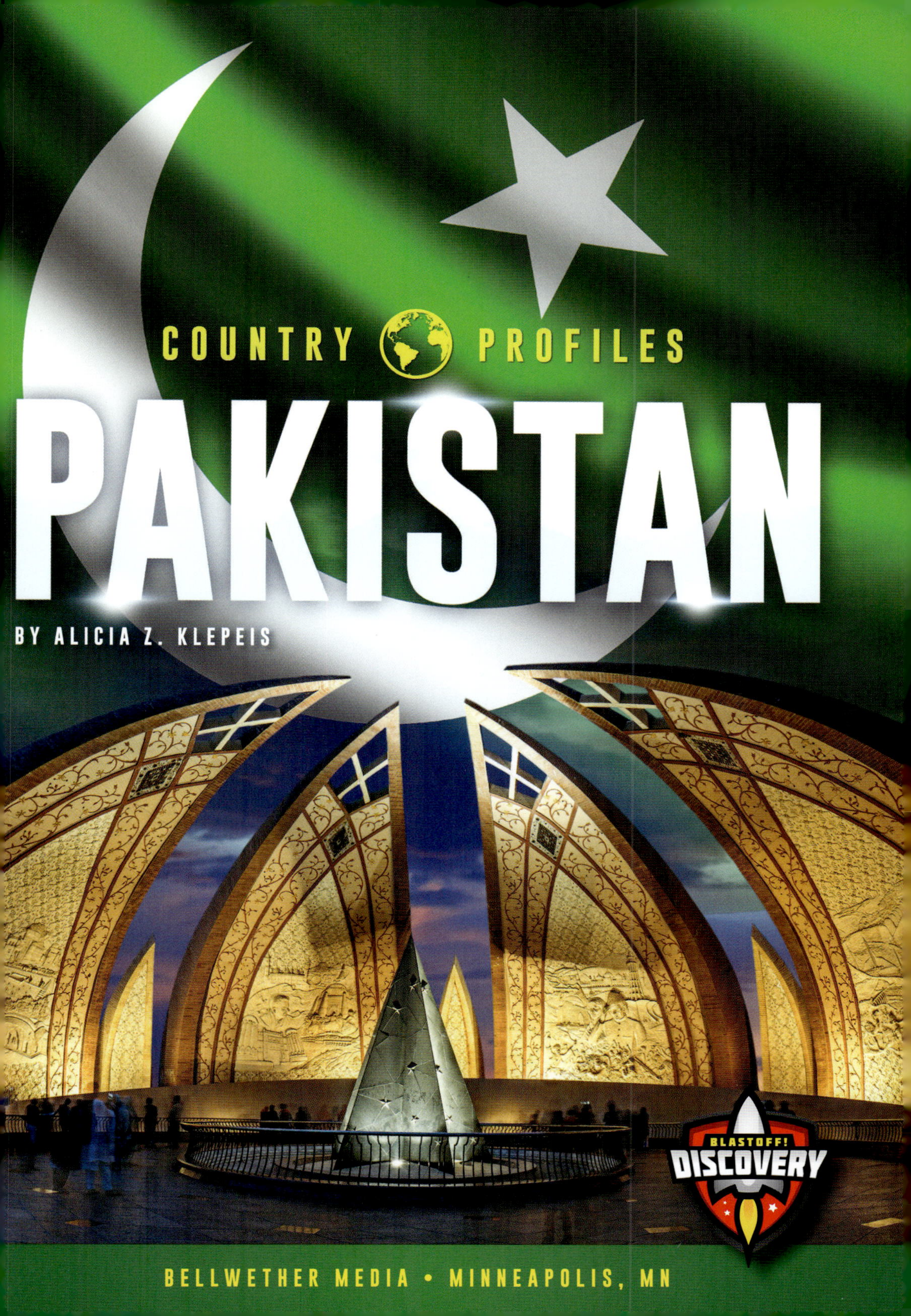

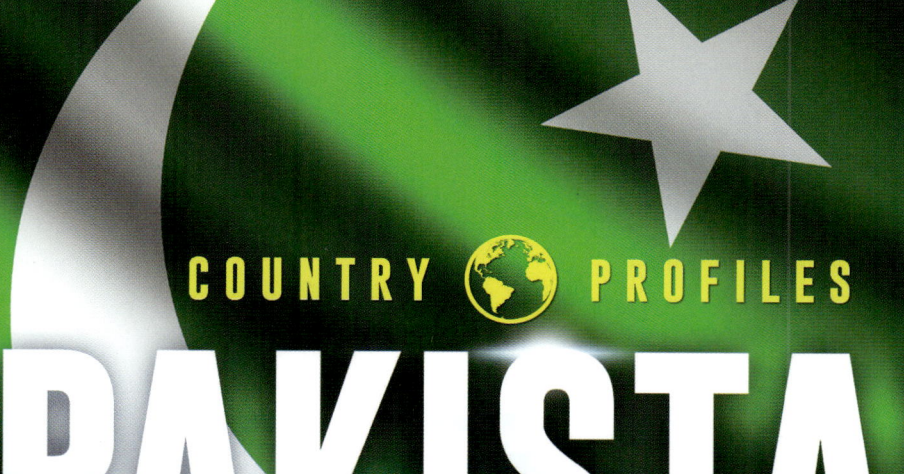

COUNTRY PROFILES

PAKISTAN

BY ALICIA Z. KLEPEIS

BLASTOFF! DISCOVERY

BELLWETHER MEDIA • MINNEAPOLIS, MN

Blastoff! Discovery launches a new mission: reading to learn. Filled with facts and features, each book offers you an exciting new world to explore!

This edition first published in 2020 by Bellwether Media, Inc.

No part of this publication may be reproduced in whole or in part without written permission of the publisher.
For information regarding permission, write to Bellwether Media, Inc., Attention: Permissions Department,
6012 Blue Circle Drive, Minnetonka, MN 55343.

Library of Congress Cataloging-in-Publication Data

Names: Klepeis, Alicia, 1971- author.
Title: Pakistan / by Alicia Z. Klepeis.
Description: Minneapolis, MN : Bellwether Media, Inc., 2020. | Series: Blastoff! Discovery | Includes bibliographical references and index. | Audience: Grades 3-8. | Audience: Ages 7-13.
Identifiers: LCCN 2019001632 (print) | LCCN 2019004955 (ebook) | ISBN 9781618915931 (ebook) | ISBN 9781644870525 (hardcover : alk. paper)
Subjects: LCSH: Pakistan–Juvenile literature. | Pakistan–Social life and customs–Juvenile literature.
Classification: LCC DS376.9 (ebook) | LCC DS376.9 .K54 2020 (print) | DDC 954.91–dc23
LC record available at https://lccn.loc.gov/2019001632

Editor: Rebecca Sabelko   Designer: Brittany McIntosh

Printed in the United States of America, North Mankato, MN.

TABLE OF CONTENTS

DEOSAI NATIONAL PARK

After bumping along on rocky roads, a family arrives at Deosai National Park. It is a sunny morning in late spring. The air is crisp. Ahead are huge mountains dusted in snow. Maybe that is why people call this area the Land of the Giants!

OTHER TOP SITES

BADSHAHI MOSQUE

BALTORO GLACIER

HINGOL NATIONAL PARK

NEELUM VALLEY

They find a path that leads through a valley full of wildflowers. They snap photos of the orange, purple, and yellow blooms. From the trail, the family sees red foxes and golden marmots. Before sunset, they eat on the edge of Sheosar Lake. Birds call to each other as they fly over its deep blue water. Welcome to Pakistan!

Pakistan is located in southern Asia. It covers 307,374 square miles (796,095 square kilometers). The capital city, Islamabad, lies on the Potwar **Plateau** in the northeastern part of the country. Many other cities, such as Lahore and Faisalabad, are located in eastern Pakistan's Punjab **province**.

Iran is Pakistan's western neighbor. Afghanistan lies to the northwest and north. China touches Pakistan on its northeast border. India is located to the east and southeast. The warm waters of the Arabian Sea wash onto the southern coast of Pakistan.

IRAN

CHINA

KASHMIR

AFGHANISTAN

ISLAMABAD - - - ★

FAISALABAD

● - - - LAHORE

PAKISTAN

INDIA

KARACHI

ARABIAN
SEA

BORDER BATTLE

Northeastern Pakistan is part of a
region called Kashmir. Pakistan,
India, and China all claim sections
of Kashmir.

LANDSCAPE AND CLIMATE

Northern Pakistan has some of the world's tallest mountains, including the Himalayas and the Karakoram Range. The Hindu Kush stretches down the country's western edge. These mountains transition into the dry and hilly Balochistan Plateau in the southwest. Toward the east, the Indus River helps give the **plains** rich soil. The Thar Desert along the border with India is a maze of sand dunes and ridges.

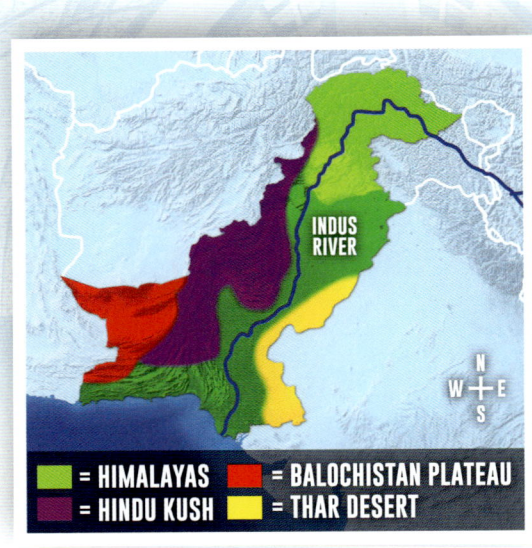

INDUS RIVER

N
W + E
S

= HIMALAYAS   = BALOCHISTAN PLATEAU
= HINDU KUSH   = THAR DESERT

THAR DESERT

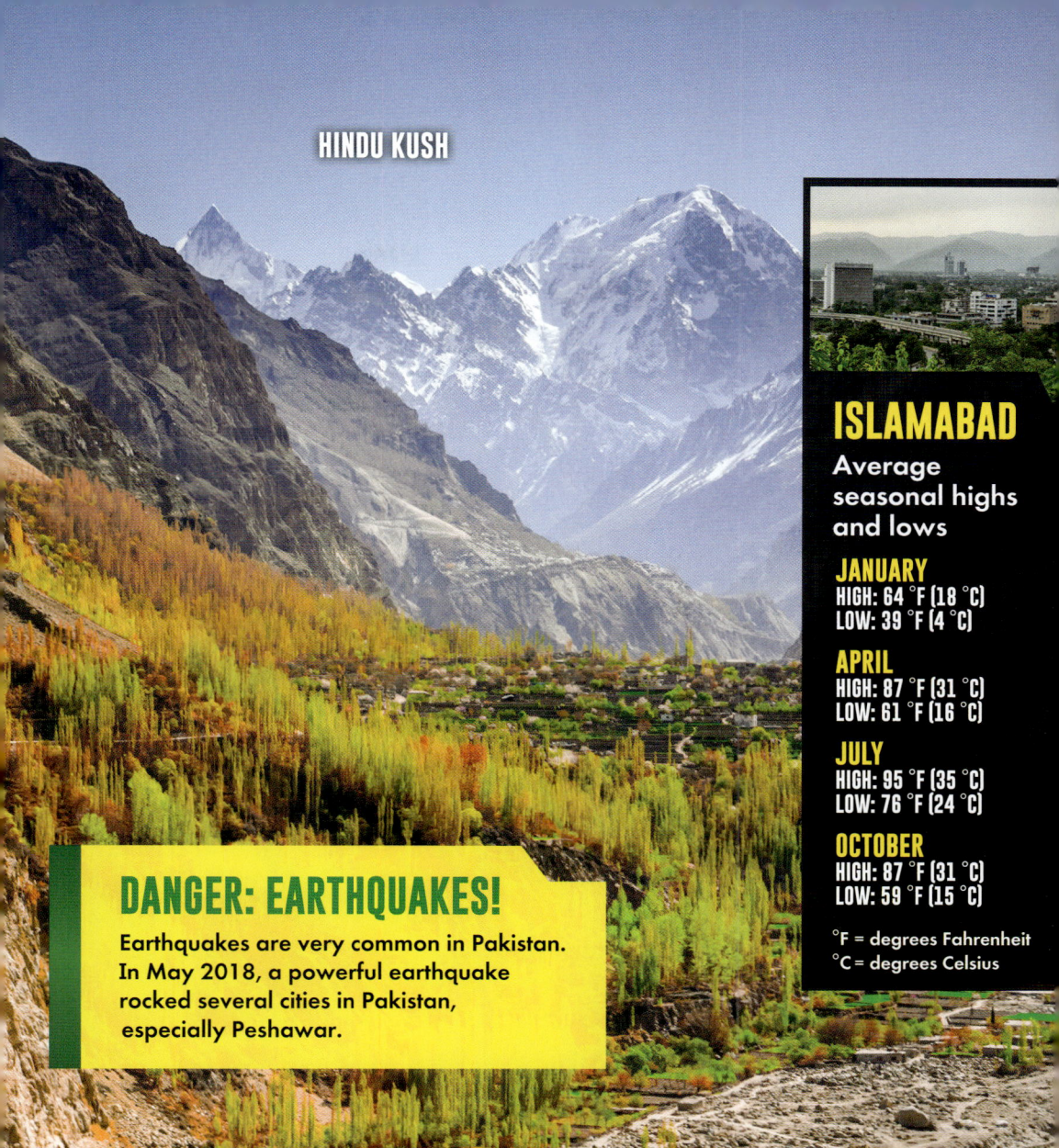

HINDU KUSH

ISLAMABAD
Average seasonal highs and lows

JANUARY
HIGH: 64 °F (18 °C)
LOW: 39 °F (4 °C)

APRIL
HIGH: 87 °F (31 °C)
LOW: 61 °F (16 °C)

JULY
HIGH: 95 °F (35 °C)
LOW: 76 °F (24 °C)

OCTOBER
HIGH: 87 °F (31 °C)
LOW: 59 °F (15 °C)

°F = degrees Fahrenheit
°C = degrees Celsius

DANGER: EARTHQUAKES!
Earthquakes are very common in Pakistan. In May 2018, a powerful earthquake rocked several cities in Pakistan, especially Peshawar.

Pakistan is in the **temperate** zone. Overall, the climate is dry. Summers are hot and winters can be cool or cold. Near the Arabian Sea, the climate is usually warm and humid.

Pakistan is home to a wide variety of wildlife. In the high mountains, snow leopards prey on goats, marmots, and wild sheep. Siberian ibex graze on mountain grasses, leaves, and twigs. Giant snakeheads swim alongside Rita catfish in the Indus River while pelicans swoop down to the river **delta** to catch a meal. **Venomous** cobras also slither nearby.

Tortoises creep along in the Thar Desert as Chinkara gazelles whiz through the landscape. In the winter, Houbara bustard birds stop in the desert as part of their annual **migration**. Giant humpback whales are sometimes spotted off Pakistan's Arabian coast.

BLACK COBRA

CHINKARA GAZELLE

HOUBARA BUSTARD

HUMPBACK WHALE

SNOW LEOPARD

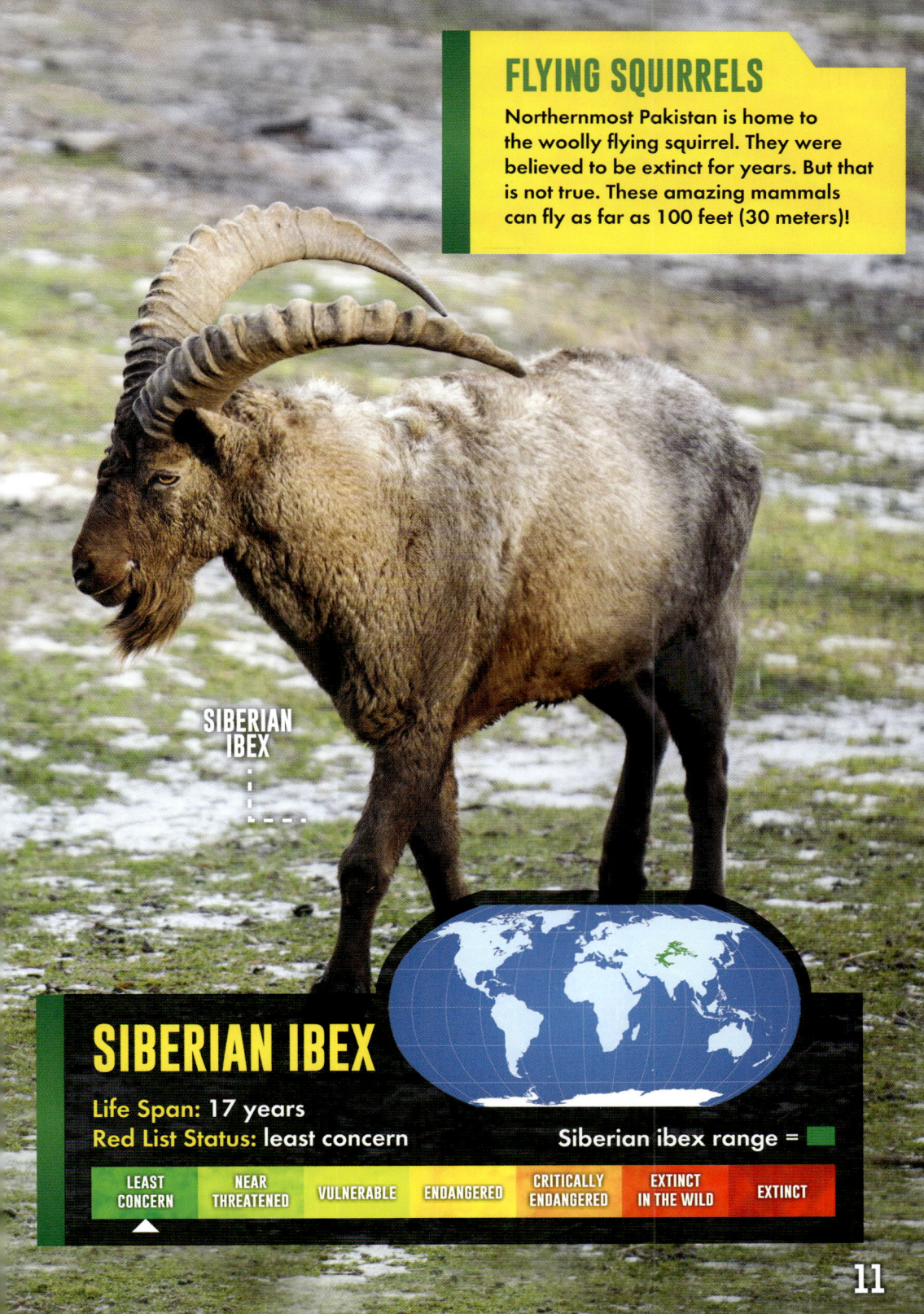

FLYING SQUIRRELS

Northernmost Pakistan is home to the woolly flying squirrel. They were believed to be extinct for years. But that is not true. These amazing mammals can fly as far as 100 feet (30 meters)!

SIBERIAN
IBEX

SIBERIAN IBEX

Life Span: 17 years
Red List Status: least concern

Siberian ibex range =

LEAST CONCERN	NEAR THREATENED	VULNERABLE	ENDANGERED	CRITICALLY ENDANGERED	EXTINCT IN THE WILD	EXTINCT

   More than 207 million people call Pakistan home. They are
from a few different **ethnic** groups. The largest group is the
Punjabi who occupy eastern Pakistan. They make up just less
than half of the country's population. The second-largest group
is the Pashtun, or Pathan. Many live near the northern part of the
Indus River. A lot of Afghan **refugees** live in camps near the
border with Afghanistan.

Almost all Pakistanis practice Islam. Most are Sunni Muslims, but a small number are Shi'ites. Pakistan has two official languages, Urdu and English. Dozens of other languages are also spoken. But no one language is spoken by the entire population.

FAMOUS FACE

Name: Malala Yousafzai
Birthday: July 12, 1997
Hometown: Mingora, Pakistan
Famous for: The youngest winner of the Nobel Peace Prize in 2014 for her work in advancing the education of all children

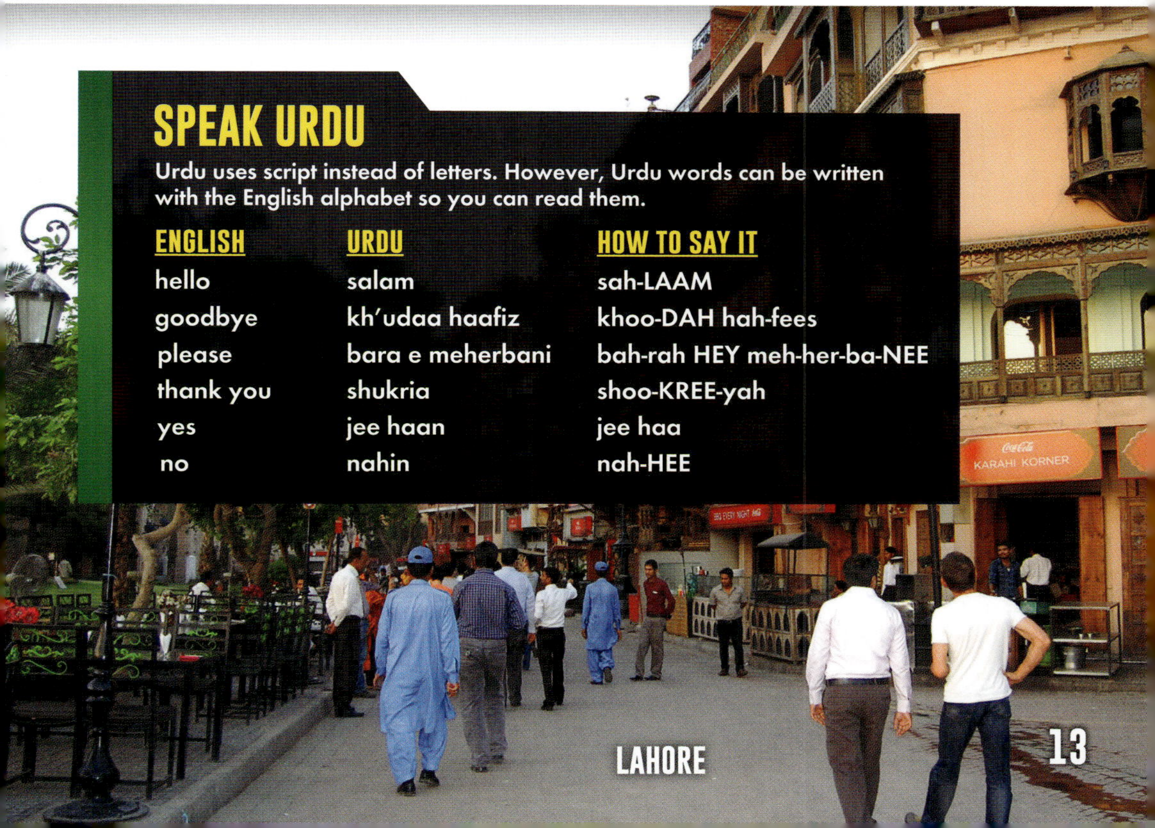

SPEAK URDU

Urdu uses script instead of letters. However, Urdu words can be written with the English alphabet so you can read them.

ENGLISH	URDU	HOW TO SAY IT
hello	salam	sah-LAAM
goodbye	kh'udaa haafiz	khoo-DAH hah-fees
please	bara e meherbani	bah-rah HEY meh-her-ba-NEE
thank you	shukria	shoo-KREE-yah
yes	jee haan	jee haa
no	nahin	nah-HEE

LAHORE

COMMUNITIES

Almost two of every three Pakistanis live in **rural** villages. Their homes are typically made of brick or mud. People often live in **compounds** close to the fields they farm. They may travel on foot, by truck, or even by donkey cart. City residents commonly live in apartments. Some live in **slums** on the outskirts of cities. They may not have access to clean water or electricity. Some people in cities use cars and buses to get around. Others travel on foot.

CROWDED KARACHI

More and more Pakistanis are moving to cities. Karachi has over 15 million people. About 45,000 workers arrive every month! There are not enough jobs or good housing for all the people in Karachi.

KARACHI

Family is important in Pakistani **culture**. Multiple generations of a family often live together. Women commonly stay home with their children.

Religion plays an important role in the daily lives of many Pakistanis. Muslims pray five times each day. Men typically pray at the **mosque** on Fridays. Women tend to worship at home.

Some Pakistanis wear Western-style clothing. Muslim women might wear a scarf around their heads. Some may wear a *burqa*. This garment covers women from head to toe. The country's national dress is the *shalwar kameez*. It consists of a long tunic and baggy trousers. Both men and women wear this dress. But women tend to wear bolder patterns and brighter colors.

SOCIALIZING SEPARATELY

It is common for friends and relatives to visit each other in Pakistan. But in some homes, men will entertain their male guests in a separate room.

SHALWAR KAMEEZ

Students in Pakistan begin school at age 5. Primary school lasts through fifth grade. Children are technically required to go to school until age 16. But very few students do. Some may work. Girls often help around the home. Students who complete middle and high school may study at university.

More than two out of five Pakistanis work in agriculture. Farmers grow cotton, wheat, sugarcane, rice, and other crops. Some Pakistanis have **service jobs**. They often work for the government in fields such as defense or construction. Other people in Pakistan **manufacture** products like clothing, construction materials, and surgical equipment.

SUGARCANE FARMER

SOCCER BALL CAPITAL

More than 100 companies make soccer balls in the Pakistani city of Sialkot. About two out of five of all the world's soccer balls are made in Sialkot's factories. These include the balls used for the 2018 FIFA World Cup matches!

19

CRICKET

Pakistan's most popular sport is cricket. It is played with a kind of bat and ball. Pakistanis love playing cricket and watching matches in stadiums and on television. Other popular sports are field hockey, tennis, and soccer. Pakistanis also enjoy a variety of card games. Many play chess and a board game called *ludo*. This strategy game, which came from India, is over a thousand years old.

LUDO

Watching TV and going to the movies are common pastimes in Pakistan. People also enjoy going to restaurants, whether for Pakistani food or pizza. Families may travel to the northern mountains for vacations.

MAKE YOUR OWN KITE

Flying kites is a popular activity in Pakistan. Try making your own!

What You Need:

- scissors
- newspaper
- two sticks
  (twigs, garden stakes, BBQ skewers)
- string
- marker

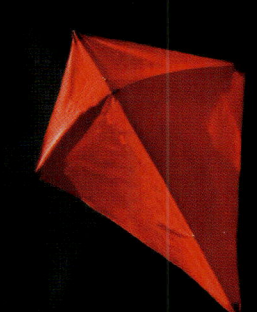

Instructions:

1. Make a cross out of your two sticks. Use your string to tie the sticks together. The horizontal stick should be a little shorter than the vertical one.

2. Tie your string around the four corners, or ends, of your cross. By doing this, your string will form the diamond shape of your kite.

3. Stretch out a piece of newspaper under your kite form. Use your marker to trace the shape of the kite onto the paper.

4. When cutting out your kite, cut an extra 2 inches (5 centimeters) all the way around the shape you just traced.

5. Spread the newspaper over your kite frame. Fold the edges over the strings and glue them down. Let the glue dry.

6. Tie a long piece of string to the cross in the middle of your kite frame.

7. Head outside and give your kite a try!

21

FOOD AND ISLAM

Certain foods and drinks are forbidden by Islamic law. For example, Muslims do not eat pork.

A **staple** of the Pakistani diet is a kind of flatbread called *chapati*. This bread is often used to soak up whatever sauces are part of a meal. A popular dish is *biryani*. It is made of rice, meat, and spices. Another well-loved dish is *aloo keema*. **Traditionally** it consists of potatoes and minced **mutton**. But some cooks use chicken or other meats.

People tend to barbeque more in northern Pakistan. Chunks of meat are cooked on skewers above an open grill. Commonly eaten fruits include watermelon, apricots, mangoes, and pomegranates. Tea with milk is the nation's most popular drink.

BIRYANI

ALOO KEEMA

NAN KHATAI COOKIES

These light and sweet cookies nearly melt in your mouth. Try this recipe with the help of an adult!

Ingredients:

3/4 cup cake flour

4 tablespoons semolina flour
   or whole-wheat flour

1/4 cup plus 3 tablespoons sugar

1/2 cup plus 2 tablespoons unsalted butter

2/3 teaspoon vanilla extract

1 egg, beaten

Steps:

1. In a big mixing bowl, beat together the butter and sugar until fluffy.

2. Add the two types of flour and the vanilla. The dough should be soft.

3. Divide the dough into 12 pieces. Roll each piece into a small ball using your hands. Flatten these slightly so they are about one inch thick.

4. Brush a little of the beaten egg onto the top of each cookie.

5. Bake the cookies for 15 minutes on a greased cookie sheet at 375 degrees Fahrenheit (191 degrees Celsius).

6. Let the cookies cool completely on a wire rack. Enjoy!

Many celebrations in Pakistan are Islamic holidays. During the month of Ramadan, Muslims **fast** from sunrise to sunset every day. The end of Ramadan is celebrated with *Eid al-Fitr*. People have large feasts with family and friends. They also do **charitable** acts and make donations to those in need.

On August 14, Pakistanis celebrate their nation's independence from Britain. People dress in green and white, the national colors. Some Pakistanis visit national monuments or attend concerts. But people in Pakistan celebrate their nation and culture all year long!

REPUBLIC DAY

On March 23, the people of Pakistan celebrate Pakistan Day. A huge parade takes place in Islamabad. The nation's president gives out awards to deserving citizens. People offer special prayers for both peace and success.

EID AL-FITR
CARNIVAL

1843
British takeover of
the Sindh region

1526-1857 CE
Mughal Empire rules over
what is now Pakistan

AROUND 2500-1700 BCE
Highly successful period
of the Indus civilization

1947
Pakistan becomes an
independent country

1988
Benazir Bhutto becomes the first female prime minister of Pakistan

2014
Malala Yousafzai becomes the youngest person to ever win the Nobel Peace Prize

2005
An earthquake destroys the Pakistani-ruled part of Kashmir and affects tens of thousands of residents

2001
President Musharraf supports the U.S. attacks on the Taliban and al-Qaeda in Afghanistan

2011
Osama bin Laden, founder of al-Qaeda, is killed in Abbottabad

PAKISTAN FACTS

Official Name: Islamic Republic of Pakistan

Flag of Pakistan: Pakistan's flag is green and white. On the left side is a white rectangle. This represents the country's religious minorities. Most of the flag is green with a white crescent and star. These shapes are symbols of Islam, Pakistan's official religion.

Area: 307,374 square miles
(796,095 square kilometers)

Capital City: Islamabad

Important Cities: Karachi, Lahore, Faisalabad

Population:
207,862,518 (2018)

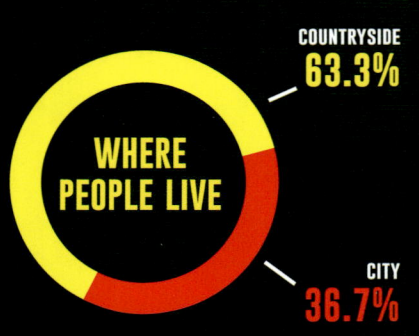

WHERE PEOPLE LIVE

COUNTRYSIDE
63.3%

CITY
36.7%

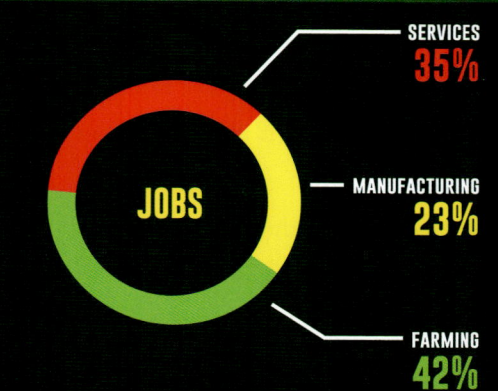

SERVICES
35%

MANUFACTURING
23%

FARMING
42%

JOBS

Main Exports:

textiles

rice

sugar

leather goods

medical equipment

National Holiday:
Pakistan Day (March 23)

Main Languages:
Punjabi, Sindhi, Saraiki, Pashto,
Urdu (official), English (official)

Form of Government:
federal parliamentary republic

Title for Country Leaders:
prime minister (head of government),
president (head of state)

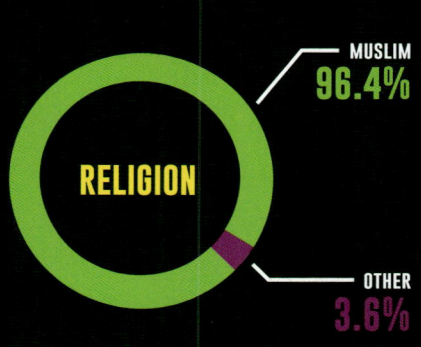

MUSLIM
96.4%

OTHER
3.6%

RELIGION

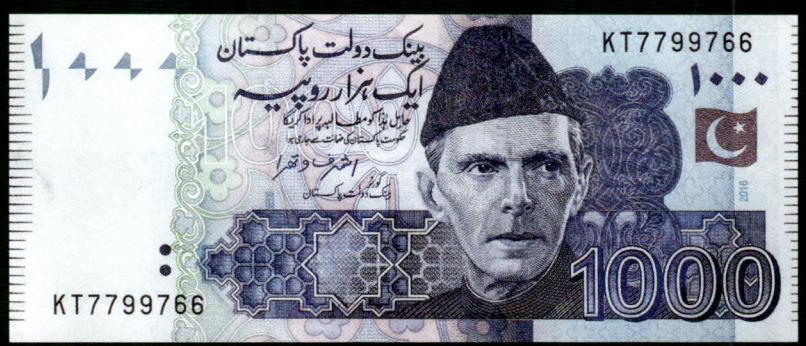

Unit of Money:
Pakistani rupee

GLOSSARY

charitable—related to being generous and kind to others

compounds—enclosed areas that include groups of buildings

culture—the beliefs, arts, and ways of life in a place or society

delta—the area around the mouth of a river

ethnic—related to a group of people who share customs and an identity

fast—to stop eating all foods or particular foods for a time

manufacture—to make products, often with machines

migration—the act of traveling from one place to another, often with the seasons

mosque—a building that Muslims use for worship

mutton—sheep meat

plains—large areas of flat land

plateau—an area of raised, flat land

province—an area within a country; provinces follow all the laws of the country and make some of their own laws.

refugees—people who flee their homes for safety

rural—related to the countryside

service jobs—jobs that perform tasks for people or businesses

slums—parts of a city that are crowded and have poor housing

staple—a widely used food or other item

temperate—associated with a mild climate that does not have extreme heat or cold

traditionally—related to the customs, ideas, or beliefs handed down from one generation to the next

venomous—producing a poisonous substance called venom

TO LEARN MORE

AT THE LIBRARY

Cantor, Rachel Anne. *Pakistan*. New York, N.Y.: Bearport Publishing, 2017.

Corey, Shana. *Malala: A Hero for All*. New York, N.Y.: Random House, 2016.

Murray, Julie. *Pakistan*. Minneapolis, Minn.: Big Buddy Books, 2015.

ON THE WEB

FACTSURFER

Factsurfer.com gives you a safe, fun way to find more information.

1. Go to www.factsurfer.com.

2. Enter "Pakistan" into the search box and click 🔍.

3. Select your book cover to see a list of related web sites.

INDEX